Wild Life LOL! ™
Elephants

Ready for some ele-FUN?

SCHOLASTIC

Library of Congress Cataloging-in-Publication Data
Title: Elephants
Description: New York, NY: Children's Press, an imprint of Scholastic Inc., 2020. | Series: Wild Life LOL! | Includes index.
Identifiers: LCCN 2019006054| ISBN 9780531240366 (library binding) | ISBN 9780531234891 (paperback)
Subjects: LCSH: Elephants—Juvenile literature.
Classification: LCC QL737.P98 E4295 2020 | DDC 599.67—dc23

Produced by Spooky Cheetah Press

Design by Anna Tunick Tabachnik

Contributing Editor and Jokester: Pamela Chanko

Printed in Heshan, China 62

SCHOLASTIC, CHILDREN'S PRESS, WILD LIFE LOL!™, and associated logos are trademarks and/or registered trademarks of
Scholastic Inc.

1 2 3 4 5 6 7 8 9 10 R 29 28 27 26 25 24 23 22 21 20

Scholastic Inc., 557 Broadway, New York, NY 10012.

Photographs ©: cover, spine: Dave King/Getty Images; cover speech bubbles and throughout: pijama61/iStockphoto; cover speech
bubbles and throughout: Astarina/Shutterstock; back cover: John Lund/Getty Images; 1: Gallo Images/Michael Poliza/Getty Images;
3 top left and throughout: John M Lund Photography Inc/Getty Images; 3 top right: Martyn Colbeck/Getty Images; 3 bottom and
throughout: Karine Aigner/Getty Images; 4: Svetlana Foote/Shutterstock; 5 child silo: Nowik Sylwia/Shutterstock; 5 elephants: Arttii
Univerz/Shutterstock; 6: goodze/iStockphoto; 7: Martyn Colbeck/Getty Images; 8-9: jez_bennett/iStockphoto; 10 top: Katja El Sol
Cemazar/Shutterstock; 10 bottom: Nick Dale/Design Pics/Getty Images; 11 top: pamelaoliveras/Getty Images; 11 bottom: fotoslaz/
Shutterstock; 12-13: 104kelly/iStockphoto; 15 left: Tony Heald/Minden Pictures; 16: FRANKHILDEBRAND/iStockphoto; 17 top left:
Lockenes/Shutterstock; 17 top right: Stephen Shepherd/Getty Images; 17 bottom left: Jean-Philippe Delobelle/Getty Images;
17 bottom right: Vincent Marion/Biosphoto; 18-19: michelle guillermin/Shutterstock; 20: Martyn Colbeck/Getty Images; 21 left:
Jlindsay/Dreamstime; 21 right: Michael Nitzschke/imageBROKER/age fotostock; 22-23: FLPA/Neil Bowman/age fotostock; 24-25:
momatarou2012/Wikipedia; 26 left: David Santiago Garcia/Getty Images; 26 right: Diptendu Dutta/AFP/Getty Images; 27 left: Carl
De Souza/AFP/Getty Images; 27 right: LMspencer/Shutterstock; 28 left: Warren Photographic/Science Source; 28 center: Nobumichi
Tamura/Stocktrek Images/Getty Images; 28 right: Jlindsay/Dreamstime; 29 left: Alain Mafart-Renodier/Biosphoto; 29 center: Africa
Media Online/Alamy Images; 29 right: James R.D. Scott/Getty Images; 30 map: Jim McMahon/Mapman®; 32: jez_bennett/iStockphoto.

TABLE OF CONTENTS

Wow! That's heavy!

MEET THE INCREDIBLE ELEPHANT

Are you ready to be amazed and amused? Keep reading! This book will make you trumpet with joy!

LoL!
What's the biggest ant on Earth? **An ELEPH-ant!**

Let's get started. I'm all ears!

At a Glance

Where do they live? → Elephants live on grasslands and in forests and desert areas.

What do they do? → Female elephants live in family groups with their young.

What do they eat? → Elephants eat leaves and branches, as well as grasses and fruit.

What do they look like? → Elephants have huge bodies with wrinkled gray skin, long trunks, and big, floppy ears.

How big are they? →

HINT: You're smaller.
Check this out:

African
11 ft.

Asian
8 ft. 11 in.

4 ft. 6 in.

Human (age 9)   Elephants (at shoulder)

TWO KINDS OF ELEPHANTS

Here's how to tell Asian and African elephants apart.

two humps on head

smallish, rounded ears

Asian

three front toes

WACKY FACT:
Female Asian elephants either don't have any tusks or have very short tusks called tushes.

live in scrub forests and rain forests in Asia

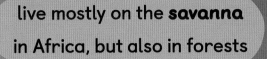

live mostly on the **savanna** in Africa, but also in forests

LOL!
What's the difference between African and Asian elephants?
About 5,000 miles!

one round dome on head

large ears

African

four front toes

savanna: a flat, grassy plain with few or no trees

AN ELEPHANT'S BODY

There is no mistaking an elephant for any other animal!

LOL!
Why is an elephant's skin so wrinkled? **It takes too long to iron it.**

Really Wrinkled

An elephant's skin is made up of thousands of folds. The folds hold water to help keep the elephant cool.

I Hear Ya!

Elephants hear noises up to $1\frac{1}{2}$ miles away! They also flap their ears to keep cool.

Turbo Trunk

An elephant's strong trunk is made up of more than 40,000 muscles. (A person's entire body has about 640 muscles!)

What Big Teeth You Have!

An elephant's tusks are actually two long teeth. The animal uses them to dig, strip bark off trees, and defend itself.

WACKY FACT: An elephant's skin is 16% of its total body weight!

THE NOSE KNOWS

Elephants have a great sense of smell. But they use their trunks for so much more!

Chow Down

Elephants pick up food with their trunks and place it in their mouths. They also suck up water in their trunks to spray it in their mouths.

Natural Sunscreen

Elephants use their trunks to toss mud and dirt over their bodies. This protects their sensitive skin from sunburn and insect bites.

WACKY FACT:
Baby elephants suck on their trunks, just like some human children suck their thumbs!

Dive In!

Elephants are very good swimmers. In deep water, they can use their trunks as snorkels to breathe.

Hugs and Kisses

Elephants often greet one another by touching with their trunks. A mother elephant may wrap her trunk around her baby to comfort it.

FAMILY MATTERS

Elephants live in large groups called herds.

THAT'S EXTREME!
In Hwange National Park in Africa, some herds have up to 350 elephants!

Roll Call
The herd is made up of adult females and their young. Young elephants are called calves. Adult females are called cows.

Has anyone seen my niece?

Taking the Lead

All the elephants in a herd are related. Females stay with their herd for life. The oldest female is the head of the family. She knows where to find food and water.

Later, Dudes

Male elephants, or bulls, stay with the herd only until they are around 12 years old.

Here I am, Auntie!

TALK LIKE AN ELEPHANT

Elephants have lots of ways to **communicate** with each other.

THAT'S EXTREME!
Scientists have identified more than 70 different elephant calls.

WACKY FACT:
An elephant's ear can weigh as much as 100 pounds.

Blow That Horn

Elephants are famous for their loud trumpet blasts. The sound may mean the elephant is excited or happy—or lost or angry.

communicate: to share information

Was that the ELE-phone ringing?

LOL!
How can you tell if an elephant is in your refrigerator? The door won't close!

Secret Sounds

Many of an elephant's sounds can't be heard by humans. These rumbles can travel up to 6 miles. Elephants actually pick up the sound vibrations through their feet!

Keep an Eye on the Ears

Elephants flutter their ears to say hello to each other. But when an elephant spreads its ears wide, it may be angry and getting ready to charge.

READY TO EAT

It takes a lot of food to make an elephant feel full! An adult can eat 200 to 600 pounds of **vegetation** and drink 50 gallons of water in a day.

THAT'S EXTREME!
Elephants produce about 250 pounds of poop a day!

WACKY FACT:
An elephant can hold about 2 gallons of water in its trunk.

Be honest: Is there food on my face?

vegetation: plant life

acacia trees

grass

These are some of an elephant's favorite foods.

baobab trees

bamboo

LOOKING FOR LOVE

When a female elephant is 10 to 12 years old, she is ready to **mate**.

1

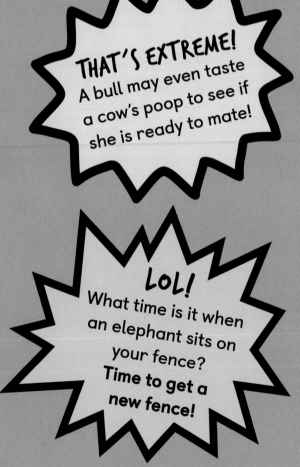

THAT'S EXTREME!
A bull may even taste a cow's poop to see if she is ready to mate!

LOL!
What time is it when an elephant sits on your fence?
Time to get a new fence!

Calling All Bulls

When a female is ready to have a baby, she sends out calls to let bulls know she is looking for a mate.

mate: to join together to have babies

2

Love Is in the Air

Bulls smell the cow's urine to tell if she is ready. The bull chases the female until she stops so they can mate.

3

A Long Wait

It will be 22 months before the baby is born. That is the longest pregnancy of any land animal.

OH, BABY

When the female is ready to give birth, the herd gathers in a circle around her. They make sure no **predators** can get near the new baby!

①

Special Delivery

A female usually has one calf every five years. A newborn weighs 200 pounds and is about 3 feet tall. The older cows help the baby stand up minutes after it is born.

predators: animals that hunt other animals for food

You're thirsty again?!

FAST FACT
Elephants can live as long as 70 years in the wild.

② Baby Food

Because elephants are **mammals**, the calf's first food is its mother's milk. The calf starts eating solid food after four months, but still drinks its mom's milk for two years.

③ Everyone Chips In

As the herd moves, the calf walks under its mother. The other elephants slow down so the baby can keep up. They also take turns babysitting!

mammals: animals that produce milk to feed their young

WORKING ELEPHANTS

Today there are more than 15,000 elephants working in Asia. They are mostly used to clear forests.

Muscle-Bound
An elephant can use its trunk to carry a log weighing up to 600 pounds.

THAT'S EXTREME!
One working elephant can carry up to 4 tons of wood per day. That's about two times as heavy as a car!

LoL!
Why do elephants need trunks? Because they don't have pockets.

Personal Trainer
Asian elephants are trained from when they are very young. Their trainers are called mahouts (ma-HOWTS).

Heave Ho!
Elephants also pull the machinery that is brought into the forest to cut down trees.

ANCIENT ELEPHANTS

It might be impossible to believe, but this is the skeleton of the oldest known **ancestor** of elephants!

THAT'S EXTREME!
Moeritherium lived more than 35 million years ago!

Combo
Moeritherium had a long body and short legs. It looked like a combination of a hippo and tapir.

ancestor: a family member who lived long ago

Small Fry
Moeritherium didn't have a long trunk. It was also much smaller than today's elephants. It reached only 29 to 42 inches tall at the shoulder.

Home, Sweet Home
This creature lived in northern Africa, both on land and in the water.

Don't you recognize me? I'm family!

Sorry, I just don't see the resemblance!

ELEPHANTS AND PEOPLE

We have a long history together!

1930s

Between five million and 10 million African elephants and about 200,000 Asian elephants lived in the wild.

1940 to 1988

Elephants' **habitats** got smaller as people moved into areas where they lived. The animals were hunted for their tusks.

habitats: the places where a plant or an animal makes its home

In Africa, officials sometimes seize and burn tusks from illegally hunted elephants.

THAT'S EXTREME! These intelligent and caring creatures have the largest brains of any land animals.

1989

Buying and selling ivory was outlawed around the world. Still, 27,000 elephants are killed for their tusks every year.

Today

About 400,000 African and 40,000 Asian elephants survive in the wild. **Conservation** groups are fighting to protect them.

conservation: the protection of nature (like forests and animals)

Elephant Cousins

The two animal relatives that look most like elephants are both extinct.

I've never seen my relatives, but I hear we look a lot alike!

mastodons

Well, hello, Grandma!

Being extinct makes it hard to go to family reunions!

woolly mammoths

Please note: Animals are not shown to scale.

Like our elephant cousins, we graze on plants . . . but we do it underwater!

dugongs

hyraxes

We don't look much like our elephant relatives—except for our wrinkled skin!

We're actually the elephant's closest living relatives!

manatees

29

The Wild Life

Check out the red areas on this map of the world. They show that elephants still live where they have always been found: Africa and Asia. However, the numbers of elephants living in those places have dropped alarmingly. If the populations continue to fall, elephants could one day become **extinct**.

Asia

Africa

extinct: no longer found alive

Protecting the Gentle Giants

It is estimated that more than 70 elephants are killed every day. Most of them are killed for their tusks. Others are killed by farmers to keep them from eating crops.

Conservation groups are working to keep elephants safe. Some organizations, like the Elephant Orphanage Project in Africa, rescue young elephants whose herd mates have been killed for their tusks. Volunteers care for the calves until they are old enough to return to the wild. Other groups teach farmers safe ways to keep elephants away from their crops instead of killing them.

What Can You do?

Talk to a trusted adult about joining Roots & Shoots, a youth program founded by Dr. Jane Goodall in 1991. You'll be joining thousands of kids around the world in helping to make the planet safer for all wildlife.

INDEX

ABOUT THIS BOOK

This book is a laugh-out-loud early-grade adaptation of *Elephants* by Anna Prokos. *Elephants* was originally published by Scholastic as part of its Nature's Children series in 2018.

Thanks a TON for reading!